DOWNSIDE OF DRUGS

Doping

Human Growth Hormone, Steroids, & Other Performance-Enhancing Drugs

DOWNSIDE OF DRUGS

ADHD Medication Abuse: Ritalin®, Adderall®, & Other Addictive Stimulants

Alcohol & Tobacco

Caffeine: Energy Drinks, Coffee, Soda, & Pills

Dangerous Depressants & Sedatives

Doping: Human Growth Hormone, Steroids, & Other Performance-Enhancing Drugs

Hard Drugs: Cocaine, LSD, PCP, & Heroin

Marijuana: Legal & Developmental Consequences

Methamphetamine & Other Amphetamines

New Drugs: Bath Salts, Spice, Salvia, & Designer Drugs

Over-the-Counter Medications

Prescription Painkillers: OxyContin®, Percocet®, Vicodin®, & Other Addictive Analgesics

DOWNSIDE OF DRUGS

Doping

Human Growth Hormone, Steroids, & Other Performance-Enhancing Drugs

Celicia Scott

Mason Crest

Mason Crest
450 Parkway Drive, Suite D
Broomall, PA 19008
www.masoncrest.com

Printed and bound in the United States of America.

9 8 7 6 5 4 3 2

Series ISBN: 978-1-4222-3015-2
ISBN: 978-1-4222-3020-6
ebook ISBN: 978-1-4222-8806-1

Cataloging-in-Publication Data on file with the Library of Congress.

Contents

INTRODUCTION

One of the best parts of getting older is the opportunity to make your own choices. As your parents give you more space and you spend more time with friends than family, you are called upon to make more decisions for yourself. Many important decisions that present themselves in the teen years may change your life. The people with whom you are friendly, how much effort you put into school and other activities, and what kinds of experiences you choose for yourself all affect the person you will become as you emerge from being a child into becoming a young adult.

One of the most important decisions you will make is whether or not you use substances like alcohol, marijuana, crystal meth, and cocaine. Even using prescription medicines incorrectly or relying on caffeine to get through your daily life can shape your life today and your future tomorrow. These decisions can impact all the other decisions you make. If you decide to say yes to drug abuse, the impact on your life is usually not a good one!

One suggestion I make to many of my patients is this: think about how you will respond to an offer to use drugs before it happens. In the heat of the moment, particularly if you're feeling some peer pressure, it can be hard to think clearly—so be prepared ahead of time. Thinking about why you don't want to use drugs and how you'll respond if you are asked to use them can make it easier to make a healthy decision when the time comes. Just like practicing a sport makes it easier to play in a big game, having thought about why drugs aren't a good fit for you and exactly what you might say to avoid them can give you the "practice" you need to do what's best for you. It can make a tough situation simpler once it arises.

In addition, talk about drugs with your parents or a trusted adult. This will both give you support and help you clarify your thinking. The decision is still yours to make, but adults can be a good resource. Take advantage of the information and help they can offer you.

Sometimes, young people fall into abusing drugs without really thinking about it ahead of time. It can sometimes be hard to recognize when you're making a decision that might hurt you. You might be with a friend or acquaintance in a situation that feels comfortable. There may be things in your life that are hard, and it could seem like using drugs might make them easier. It's also natural to be curious about new experiences. However, by not making a decision ahead of time, you may be actually making a decision without realizing it, one that will limit your choices in the future.

When someone offers you drugs, there is no flashing sign that says, "Hey, think about what you're doing!" Making a good decision may be harder because the "fun" part happens immediately while the downside—the damage to your brain and the rest of your body—may not be obvious right away. One of the biggest downsides of drugs is that they have long-term effects on your life. They could reduce your educational, career, and relationship opportunities. Drug use often leaves users with more problems than when they started.

Whenever you make a decision, it's important to know all the facts. When it comes to drugs, you'll need answers to questions like these: How do different drugs work? Is there any "safe" way to use drugs? How will drugs hurt my body and my brain? If I don't notice any bad effects right away, does that mean these drugs are safe? Are these drugs addictive? What are the legal consequences of using drugs? This book discusses these questions and helps give you the facts to make good decisions.

Reading this book is a great way to start, but if you still have questions, keep looking for the answers. There is a lot of information on the Internet, but not all of it is reliable. At the back of this book, you'll find a list of more books and good websites for finding out more about this drug. A good website is teens.drugabuse.gov, a site compiled for teens by the National Institute on Drug Abuse (NIDA). This is a reputable federal government agency that researches substance use and how to prevent it. This website does a good job looking at a lot of data and consolidating it into easy-to-understand messages.

What if you are worried you already have a problem with drugs? If that's the case, the best thing to do is talk to your doctor or another trusted adult to help figure out what to do next. They can help you find a place to get treatment.

Drugs have a downside—but as a young adult, you have the power to make decisions for yourself about what's best for you. Use your power wisely!

—*Joshua Borus, MD*

1. WHAT IS DOPING?

Doping is when athletes use drugs to improve their performance. It's any kind of drug that could give them an advantage over other *competitors* in their sport.

Doping doesn't necessarily mean the athlete is taking illegal drugs. Doping might also mean taking natural chemicals and substances, as well legal drugs and certain *supplements*. It's taking anything that will *enhance* the athlete's performance on the court, field, or track.

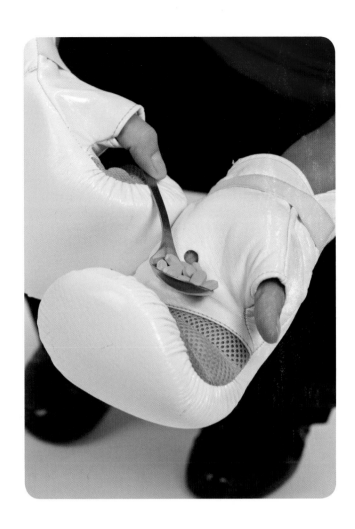

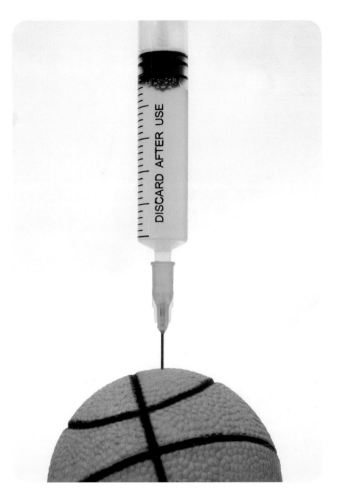

Over the past decade, the U.S. Anti-Doping Agency has *sanctioned* athletes from pretty much every sport: cyclists and soccer players, water poloists and weightlifters, rowers and wrestlers, boxers and archers, baseball players and track-and-field athletes have all been found guilty of doping.

Professional players use performance-enhancing drugs. So do Olympic athletes. And so do high school athletes. A study done in 2012 by the U.S. government found that about 1 out of every 31 high school students have used steroids at least once without a doctor's *prescription*. Many more have used some other form of doping.

2. WHAT IS THE DOWNSIDE OF DOPING?

Anything you put inside your body can change the way your body works. Some of these changes you may have wanted—but others you may not want. That's what happens when you take performance-enhancing drugs.

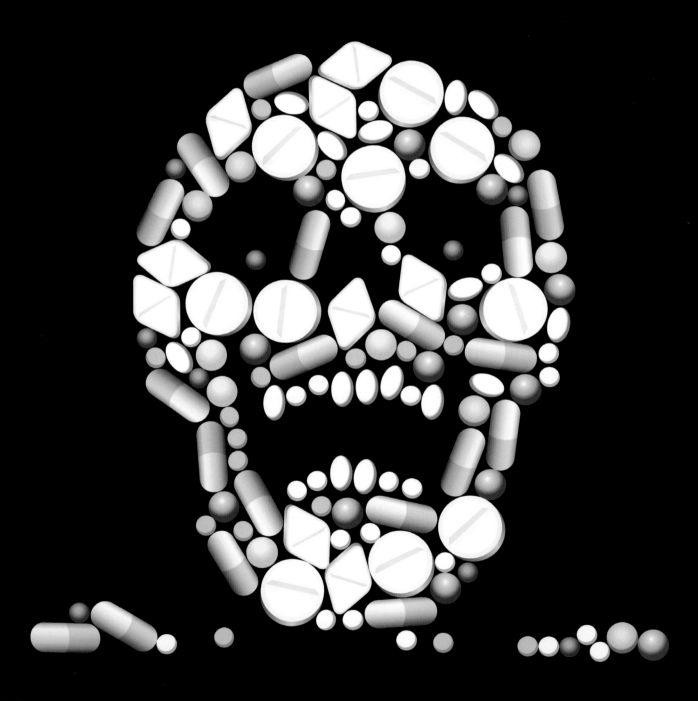

Some of these unwanted side effects can be unpleasant. Others can be dangerous. And some might kill you. That's a pretty serious downside!

Besides the risk to your life and health, there's another downside to doping: it's against the rules of pretty much every sport. If you get caught doping, you could never compete again as an athlete.

3. WHY DO ATHLETES TAKE PERFORMANCE-ENHANCING DRUGS?

Many athletes feel a lot of pressure to perform well. They face pressure from fans, coaches and managers, family members, and themselves to constantly improve their skill, strength, and speed. They want to be the best.

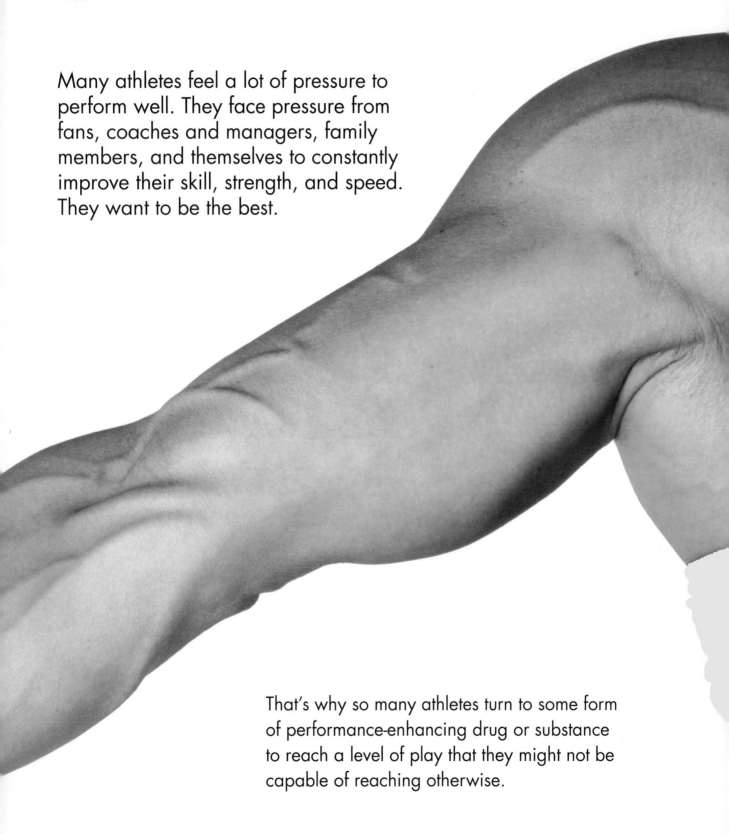

That's why so many athletes turn to some form of performance-enhancing drug or substance to reach a level of play that they might not be capable of reaching otherwise.

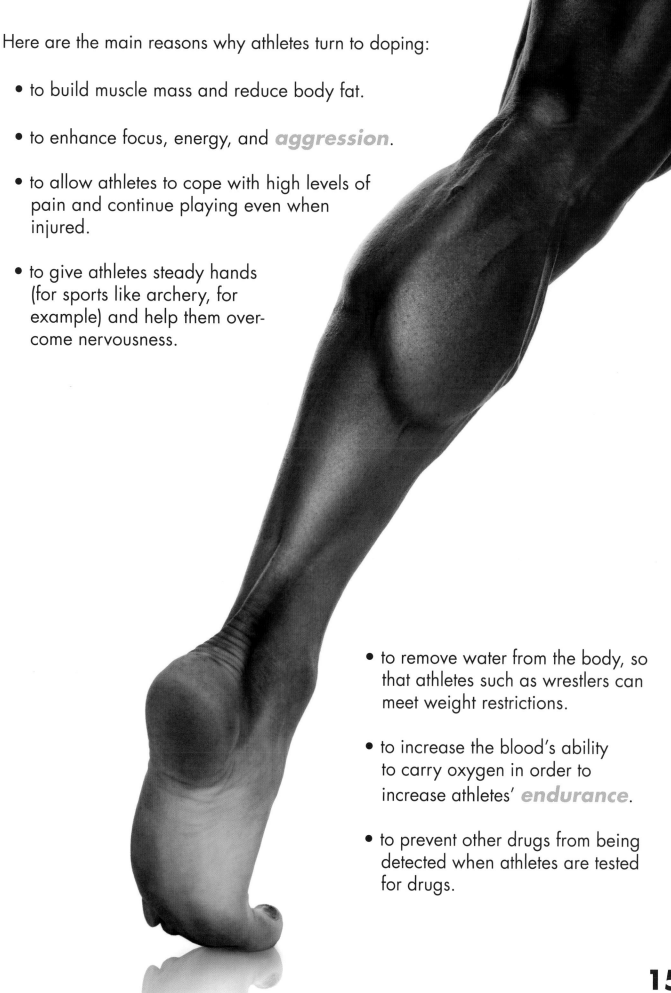

Here are the main reasons why athletes turn to doping:

- to build muscle mass and reduce body fat.

- to enhance focus, energy, and *aggression*.

- to allow athletes to cope with high levels of pain and continue playing even when injured.

- to give athletes steady hands (for sports like archery, for example) and help them overcome nervousness.

- to remove water from the body, so that athletes such as wrestlers can meet weight restrictions.

- to increase the blood's ability to carry oxygen in order to increase athletes' *endurance*.

- to prevent other drugs from being detected when athletes are tested for drugs.

15

- **Anabolic steroids** build muscle and increase endurance. They're popular with football players and weightlifters. Around three million Americans abuse anabolic steroids, and 10 percent of these are teenagers.

- Many athletes believe that **human growth hormone** (also known as gonadotropin) will improve their muscle mass and performance, while making them more *resistant* to injuries. Athletes competing in power sports, bodybuilding, professional wrestling, mixed martial arts, swimming, baseball, strength sports, track-and-field, cycling, soccer, weightlifting, skiing, and endurance sports have all been reported to abuse human growth hormone.

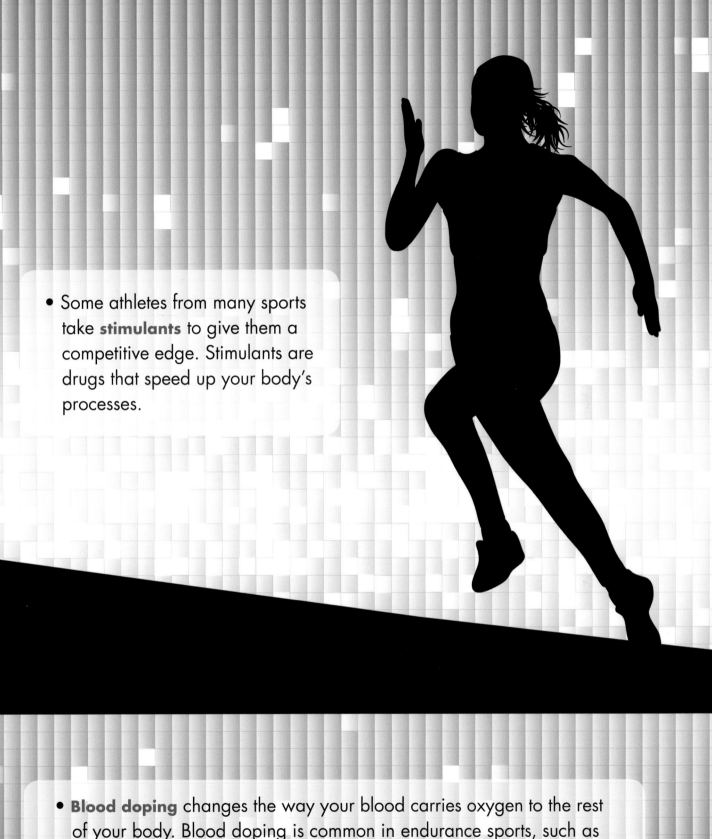

- Some athletes from many sports take **stimulants** to give them a competitive edge. Stimulants are drugs that speed up your body's processes.

- **Blood doping** changes the way your blood carries oxygen to the rest of your body. Blood doping is common in endurance sports, such as boxing, cycling, rowing, distance running, race walking, snowshoeing, cross-country skiing, and biathlons and triathlons.

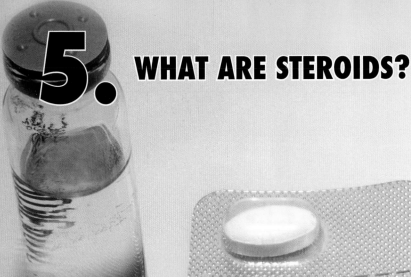

5. WHAT ARE STEROIDS?

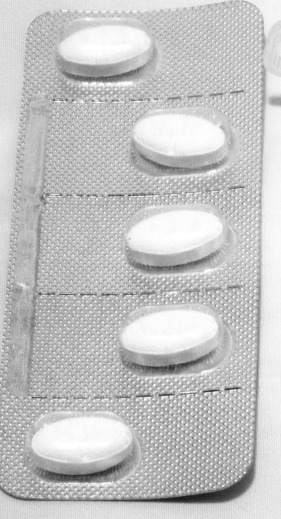

Anabolic steroids are *synthetic* versions of testosterone, the male *hormone* that makes men more muscular. They can be taken orally, *injected*, or absorbed through the skin through creams and gels. They're illegal without a doctor's prescription, and they're banned by sports organizations.

Steroid precursors are drugs the body changes into anabolic steroids. Like anabolic steroids, most of the precursors are illegal without a doctor's prescription. One of these, dehydroepiandrosterone (DHEA), is sold as an over-the-counter pill—but it's still banned by sports organizations.

Athletes sometimes take designer steroids, which have been made specifically so that they won't show up on drug tests. They have no approved medical use. Because of this, they haven't been tested or approved by the Food and Drug Administration (FDA), which could make them even more dangerous than regular steroids.

6. WHY ARE STEROIDS SO DANGEROUS?

Steroids allow athletes to train harder, recover quicker, and build muscle mass. In addition, some athletes may like the aggressive feelings they get when they take the drugs. But here's their downside:

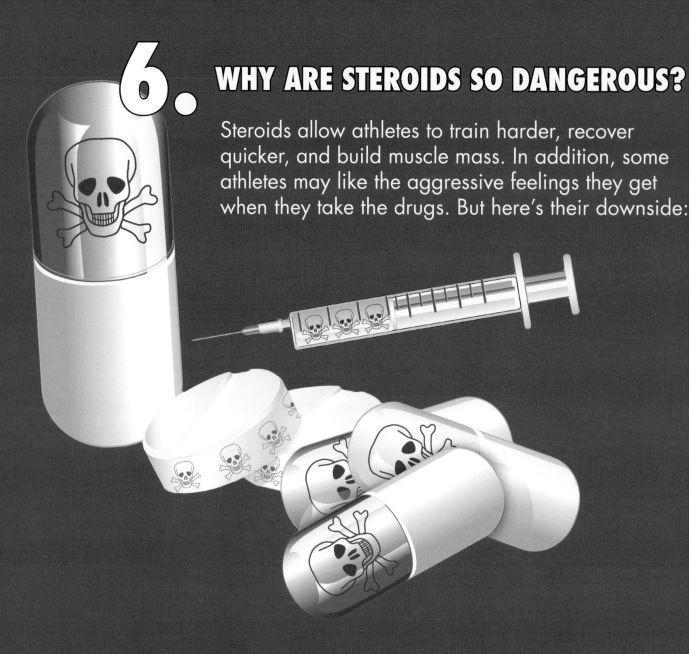

- They give you acne—really bad acne.
- They make you bald.
- They increase your risk of liver disease.
- They give you mood swings.
- They make you prone to bursts of rage and violence.
- They can make you **depressed**, to the point that you may want to kill yourself.
- They can give you high cholesterol, which increases your risk of high blood pressure and heart problems.
- They can make your **tendons** more likely to become sore or even break.
- If you're a teenager, they can keep you from growing normally.
- They are **addictive**.

Male athletes who take steroids could also:

- have their testicles (their balls) shrink.
- grow breasts.
- lose their sex drive.
- lower the number of sperm they make.

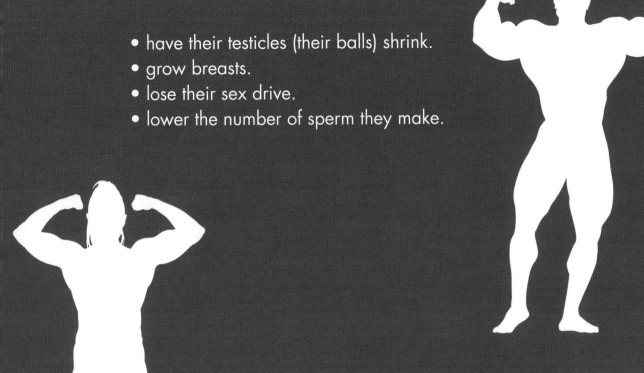

Women athletes who take steroids may:

- get deep voices.
- grow facial hair, as well as more hair on the rest of their bodies.
- have their menstrual cycles messed up.

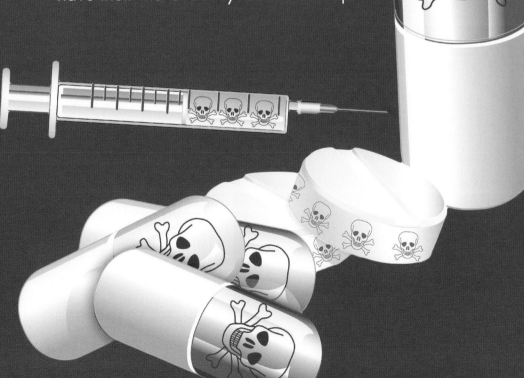

7. WHAT IS HUMAN GROWTH HORMONE?

Human growth hormone (HGH) is a chemical that your pituitary gland makes. It's what tells children's and adolescents' bodies to grow. It also helps to regulate body composition, body fluids, muscle and bone growth, sugar and fat *metabolism*, and possibly heart function.

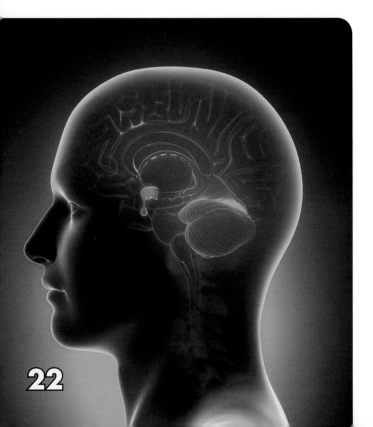

Your pituitary gland is at the center of your skull. It's only about the size of a pea, but it has a big job. It controls many important body functions, including growth and sexual development.

HGH can now be produced synthetically. It's used in a number of prescription drugs to treat several health problems.

Athletes use it because they believe it will build muscles and give them greater endurance. They get HGH shots illegally. Scientists aren't sure that HGH actually helps either strength or endurance, though.

8. WHY IS HGH DANGEROUS?

HGH (human growth hormone) may possibly make muscles and bones stronger and bigger—but it can also make other parts of your body bigger. Using HGH may give you a protruding forehead, brow, skull, and jaw. You could end up looking like a caveman for the rest of your life!

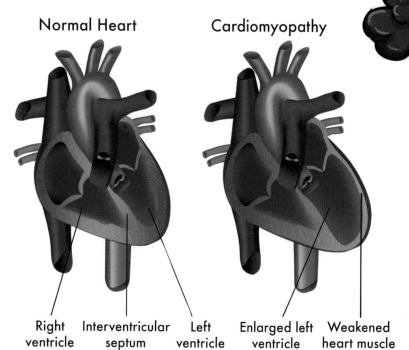

Normal Heart   Cardiomyopathy

Right | Interventricular | Left | Enlarged left | Weakened
ventricle | septum | ventricle | ventricle | heart muscle

HGH can also make your heart bigger, a condition that's called cardiomyopathy. It can cause high blood pressure and even heart failure.

HGH could damage your liver. Your liver is a large organ in the center of your body, which you need to digest your food properly. You can't live without your liver!

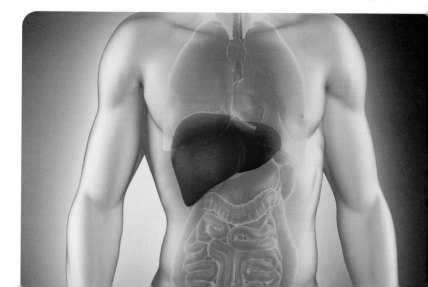

Here are some other problems caused by HGH:

- joint pain, including crippling *arthritis*

- muscle weakness

- *fluid retention* (which can make you look puffy when it's mild, and keep your body's systems from working well when it's more severe)

- carpal tunnel syndrome, a disorder in the wrist that can cause pain and numbness in the hand and fingers

- problems with blood sugar, including diabetes, which is a serious disease

- high cholesterol, which can cause other health problems

9. WHAT IS BLOOD DOPING?

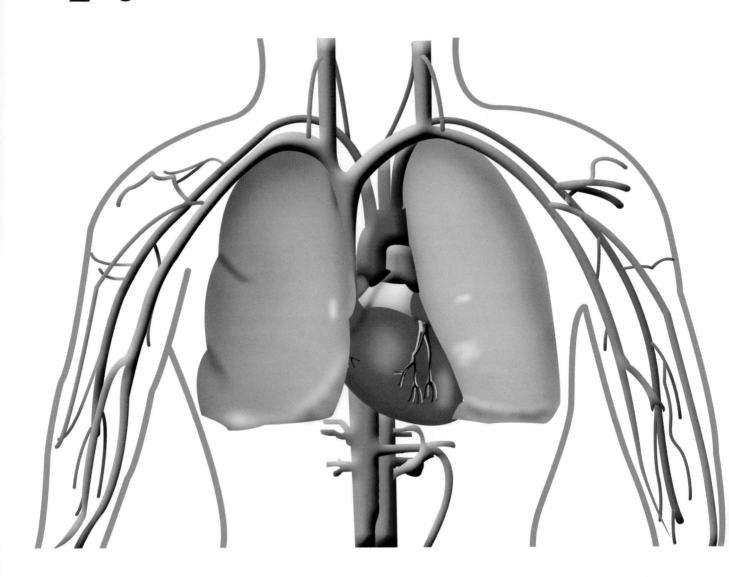

When an athlete is exercising, the heart and lungs work hard to deliver more oxygen through the blood to the body's muscles. But there is only so much the body can do. Blood doping is a way of pushing past the body's normal limits for oxygen delivery. Athletes use blood doping as a way to improve their endurance, so that they can keep running, cycling, swimming, or playing longer than they would have been able to otherwise. Blood transfusions and a chemical called EPO are two forms of blood doping.

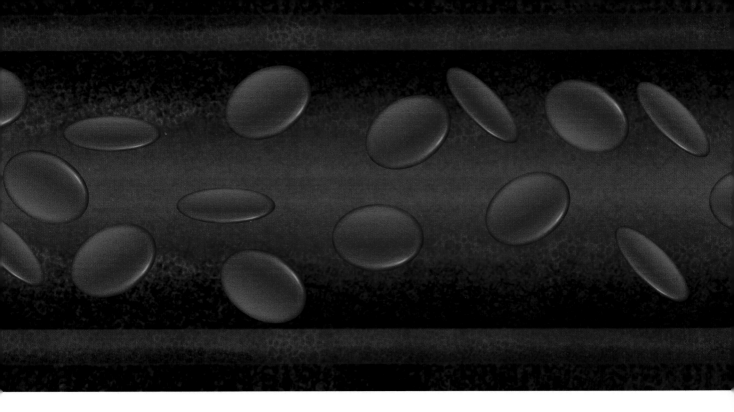

Blood transfusions—where additional blood is put into an athlete's veins—is one way to put more red blood cells into a person's blood. The red blood cells are what carry oxygen to the muscles, so if there are more red blood cells, more oxygen gets to the muscles. Athletes who use this method of blood doping usually have their own blood taken out, stored, and then put back into their bodies before a competition.

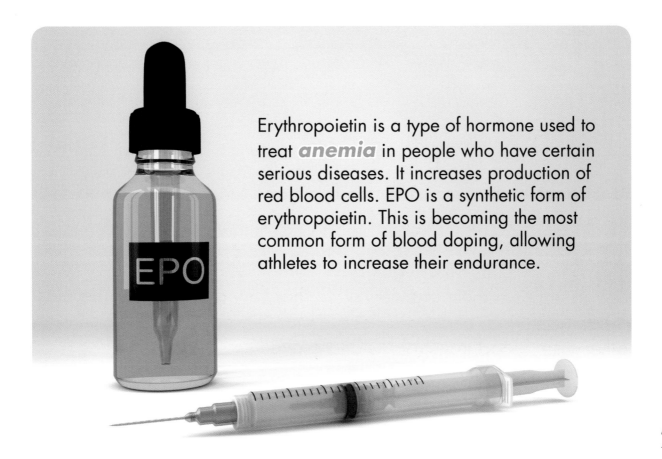

Erythropoietin is a type of hormone used to treat *anemia* in people who have certain serious diseases. It increases production of red blood cells. EPO is a synthetic form of erythropoietin. This is becoming the most common form of blood doping, allowing athletes to increase their endurance.

10. WHY IS BLOOD DOPING DANGEROUS?

Putting more blood into your blood vessels than your body can handle can cause a variety of problems, including an increased risk of heart failure, *stroke*, kidney damage, and high blood pressure. EPO can make your blood thick and sticky. Trying to pump blood that's as thick as honey is hard work for your heart. It can make you feel weak. You're more likely to have a heart attack.

Any time you put something into your blood using a needle, you run the risk of infection. Since blood doping is illegal, you can't be sure that the needles are germ free. You could catch a serious disease like HIV/AIDS or *hepatitis*.

EPO can cause sudden death during sleep. During the past twenty years, this killed at least eighteen cyclists who injected EPO so that they could cycle longer and faster.

29

11. WHAT ARE OTHER PERFORMANCE-ENHANCING DRUGS AND SUBSTANCES?

- **Androstenedione (andro)** is a hormone that's produced in the body and normally turned into testosterone in both men and women. Andro is available legally only in prescription form, but its manufacturers and bodybuilding magazines claim it allows athletes to train harder and recover more quickly. Researchers have found that these claims aren't true.

- **Amphetamines**, **meth**, and **cocaine** are illegal drugs that some athletes take to give them more energy.

- **Ephedrine** is a stimulant that's been banned by the FDA. Athletes use it to get more energy, lose weight, and make themselves more alert.

- High school athletes often take **Ritalin**®, another stimulant. Doctors prescribe it to help kids with attention-deficit/hyperactivity disorder (ADHD).

- **Painkillers** allow athletes to keep playing even when they're hurting. These drugs can also increase oxygen supply to muscle cells.

- Sedatives such as **tranquilizers** and **marijuana** are sometimes used in sports that require steady hands. Athletes may also use these drugs to help them cope with pre-game jitters.

- **Modafini** is a drug that was created to treat people who have sleep disorders. It makes people more wide awake. Athletes sometimes use it because it helps them keep exercising longer.

12. WHY ARE THESE OTHER PERFORMANCE-ENHANCING DRUGS DANGEROUS?

Here's the downside for all these other forms of doping:

- Andro turns into estrogen, the main female hormone. So if you're a guy, instead of getting big muscles, you might end up with breasts. Your balls might get smaller. Whether you're a girl or a guy, it will give you pimples, and it can make your hair fall out. Your cholesterol levels go up, making you more at risk for a heart attack or a stroke.

- All stimulants, including amphetamines, meth, ephedrine, and Ritalin, make your heart beat faster and your blood pressure increase. This could give you a heart attack or stroke, especially when you're exercising.

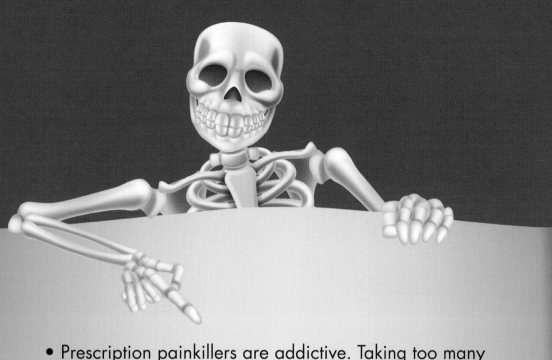

- Prescription painkillers are addictive. Taking too many can put you in a *coma*—or kill you. Even over-the-counter painkillers like Tylenol® (acetaminophen) and Advil® (ibuprofen), if taken too often, can increase your risk of a heart attack.

- Some sedatives are addictive. Taking too many can slow down your body to the point that you lose consciousness—or die.

- Modafini could give you a rash, a fever, or diarrhea. It could also damage your liver and your heart.

13. WHAT NUTRITIONAL SUPPLEMENTS DO ATHLETES USE—AND WHY CAN THEY BE A PROBLEM?

Many athletes, especially high school athletes, use nutritional supplements they believe will give them stronger bodies and improve their performance. Here are a few of them.

Creatine is an over-the-counter supplement, often used by teen athletes. It's popular with high school students who participate in football, gymnastics, hockey, and wrestling because it can increase muscle mass, help the muscles recover more quickly after exercise, and help athletes who need bursts of speed and energy. Creatine is a protein that is naturally found in your body's muscle cells. When taken in larger doses than is found in the body, creatine can increase the rate of protein *synthesis* within your cells, giving you more energy and power. However, creatine does not have the same effect for everyone. Between 20 to 30 percent of athletes don't respond to creatine supplements. Because not enough research has been done into creatine's side effects, most doctors recommend that athletes who are seventeen or younger not take creatine.

Athletes sometimes use **caffeine** to improve their performance. Caffeine is a stimulant, so it can make you feel energized and more alert. However, too much can make you jittery. It can make your heart beat too fast. The National Collegiate Athletic Association has banned high levels of caffeine in an athlete's urine. These levels are more than what an athlete could get from drinking a few cups of coffee or cola. You could only get that much caffeine in your urine from taking caffeine tablets or *suppositories*.

Ginseng is an *herb* found in Asia that is said to increase alertness and energy. Higher doses can increase body temperature, make the heart beat too fast, and cause insomnia. No scientific evidence has proven that ginseng provides any benefits to athletes.

Remember, just because these substances may be "natural" or seem harmless, anything that's labeled as a supplement hasn't been tested by the FDA the way medications have. This means you can't always know exactly what's in a supplement.

14. WHAT ABOUT "HEALTHY" THINGS, LIKE VITAMINS AND PROTEIN POWDERS?

Sometimes athletes take large doses of vitamins, thinking that vitamins will make them stronger and faster. Your body does need vitamins—but the best way to get them is from a healthy diet. Fruits and vegetables are good sources of vitamins.

Taking a multivitamin won't hurt you, and it could make up for anything you might lack in your diet. Never take more than the recommended amount, though. Some vitamins can be bad for you if you take too much of them. An overdose of vitamin B6 can damage your nerves. Vitamin E overdoses cause blood clots, *tumors*, tiredness, and problems with your reproductive system. Too much Vitamin A can make you tired and give you dry and itchy skin. When it comes to vitamins, there is such thing as too much of a good thing!

As for protein, your body needs it every day to be healthy. Eating protein immediately after a workout is also a good idea. The protein helps your muscles repair themselves after any damage. A protein shake can be a convenient way to get the protein that builds strong muscles.

However, some doctors are concerned that young athletes could be consuming too many protein supplements. Protein shakes can contain a lot of sugar and other ingredients that could lead to weight gain. And like the supplements we've already talked about, they're not regulated by the FDA, so you can't always be exactly sure what's in them. Experts say that a better way to get the protein athletes need is from a balanced diet that includes foods like lean chicken, tuna fish, beans, cottage cheese, and hard-boiled eggs.

15. IS DOPING AGAINST THE LAW?

Sports organizations have banned all performance-enhancing drugs. Besides being against sports rules, many of these drugs are illegal without a prescription. The law takes doping very seriously. If caught, you could end up doing prison time.

The fact that these drugs are against the law means that if you use them, what you're taking was made in other countries and smuggled in—or it was made in illegal labs. Either way, you can't be sure exactly what you're getting. That shot or pill you think will make you strong could be **laced** with other substances, including things that could kill you.

Athletes who get caught doping lose their reputations. They can destroy their entire careers. It's just not worth it!

16. WHAT HAPPENED TO FAMOUS ATHLETES WHO GOT CAUGHT DOPING? (WAS IT REALLY THAT BAD?)

After denying doping charges for years, Lance Armstrong finally admitted that he was guilty. He was banned for life from any sport that follows the World Anti-Doping Code. He was also stripped of his seven Tour de France titles, and he had to give back all his earnings from races.

The first woman to win five medals (three gold, two bronze) at the Sydney Olympics in 2000, track superstar Marion Jones, tested positive for performance-enhancing drugs. She pleaded guilty to federal charges and was stripped of her medals in 2007. She was also banned from the 2008 Beijing Olympics and sentenced to six months in prison and two years of probation.

Baseball player Barry Bonds had won countless awards and set records when he found himself facing legal charges for using steroids and lying about it. Instead of ending up in the Baseball Hall of Fame, he will forever be remembered as someone who cheated and lied.

Lyle Alzado started using steroids in college and never stopped until he found out he had cancer. Alzado was certain the drugs were responsible for his cancer. At the height of his steroid and human growth hormone abuse, Alzado said he spent about $30,000 a year on the drugs. His bouts of violent rage, caused by his steroid use, destroyed his marriage. He died at age forty-three, a symbol of the dangers of steroid abuse.

These athletes found out that the downside of doping is far greater than any benefits you might get!

FURTHER READING

Assael, Shaun. *Steroid Nation: Juiced Home Run Totals and a Hercules in Every High School.* New York: Permanent Tourist, 2013.

Chris, Cooper. *Run, Swim, Throw, Cheat: The Science Behind Drugs in Sport.* New York: Oxford University Press, 2012.

Fainaru-Wada, Mark and Lance Williams. *Game of Shadows: Barry Bonds and the Steroid Scandal that Rocked Professional Sports.* New York: Penguin, 2006.

Jendrick, Nathan. *Dunks, Doubles, Doping: How Steroids Are Killing American Athletes.* Guilford, CT: Lyons, 2006.

Jones, Marion. *On the Right Track: From Olympic Downfall to Finding Forgiveness and the Strength to Overcome and Succeed.* New York: Simon and Schuster, 2010.

Macur, Juliet. *Cycle of Lies: The Fall of Lance Armstrong.* New York: Harper Collins, 2014.

Moller, Verner. *Ethics of Doping and Anti-Doping: Redeeming the Soul of Sport?* New York: Routledge, 2009.

Voet, Willy. *Breaking the Chain: Drugs and Cycling.* New York: Vintage, 2011.

FIND OUT MORE ON THE INTERNET

Anabolic Steroids
www.drugabuse.gov/publications/drugfacts/anabolic-steroids

Blood Doping
www.webmd.com/fitness-exercise/blood-doping

Human Growth Hormone
www.webmd.com/fitness-exercise/human-growth-hormone-hgh

Side Effects of Blood Doping
www.medicinenet.com/script/main/art.asp?articlekey=167247

Teen Athletes and Peformance-Enhancing Drugs
www.philly.com/philly/blogs/healthy_kids/Teen-athletes-and-performance-enhancing-drugs-a-lose-lose-situation.html

United States Anti-Doping Agency
www.usada.org/publications-policies

World Anti-Doping Agency
www.wada-ama.org

GLOSSARY

addictive: Having to do with a drug that makes a person's body need that drug in order to function. When a drug is addictive, the person will need to take more and more of that drug in order to get the same results, and she won't be able to easily stop taking it.

aggression: Hostile, violent, or angry behavior toward another person.

anemia: When your blood doesn't have enough red blood cells to carry oxygen to the rest of your body.

arthritis: Painfully inflamed and stiff joints.

coma: Deep unconsciousness that you can't wake up from.

competitors: Other people that you are trying to win against.

depressed: Feeling deeply sad and hopeless, often for a long time.

endurance: The ability to keep exercising for a long time without stopping.

enhance: Make better.

fluid retention: Keeping too much water in your body instead of losing it through sweat and urine.

hepatitis: A group of diseases characterized by liver inflammation and damage.

herb: Any plant used as food, medicine, flavoring, or perfume.

hormone: Chemicals released in your body that affect how you grow and feel.

injected: Put straight into the bloodstream, usually with a hypodermic needle (a shot).

laced: Had a small amount of something else mixed in.

metabolism: The processes by which your body breaks down food and other chemicals.

over-the-counter: Drugs that you can legally buy without a prescription.

prescription: A note written by a doctor that says you need a certain medication, and gives you permission to buy it.

resistant: Able to withstand something.

sanctioned: Gave a penalty to or disciplined in some other way for breaking a rule.

side effects: Effects that a drug has on your body other than the desired effects. Usually, side effects are not good.

stroke: A blocked or burst blood vessel in the brain, which can cause brain damage.

supplements: A pill taken to replace any nutrients missing from a person's diet.

suppositories: Drugs inserted into a person's anus or vagina to be absorbed by the body.

synthesis: Creation or production.

synthetic: Artifically made.

tendons: Stetchy bands that connect your muscles to your skeleton.

tumors: Abnormal growths in your body that can be caused by cancer.

INDEX

PICTURE CREDITS

ABOUT THE AUTHOR AND THE CONSULTANT

CELICIA SCOTT lives in upstate New York. She worked in teaching before starting a second career as a writer.

DR. JOSHUA BORUS, MD, MPH, graduated from the Harvard Medical School and the Harvard School of Public Health. He completed a residency in pediatrics and then served as chief resident at Floating Hospital for Children at Tufts Medical Center before completing a fellowship in Adolescent Medicine at Boston Children's Hospital. He is currently an attending physician in the Division of Adolescent and Young Adult Medicine at Boston Children's Hospital and an instructor of pediatrics at Harvard Medical School.